Extreme Cars

# ROADSTERS

Steve Rendle

PowerKiDS press.

New York

Published in 2022 by The Rosen Publishing Group, Inc.
29 East 21st Street, New York, NY 10010

Originally Published in English by Haynes Publishing under the title: Extreme Cars Pocket Manual © Haynes Publishing 2019



Cataloging-in-Publication Data

Names: Rendle, Steve.
Title: Roadsters / Steve Rendle.
Description: New York : PowerKids Press, 2022. | Series: Extreme cars | Includes glossary and index.
Identifiers: ISBN 9781725332454 (pbk.) | ISBN 9781725332478 (library bound) | ISBN 9781725332461 (6 pack) | ISBN 9781725332485 (ebook)
Subjects: LCSH: Sports cars--Juvenile literature.
Classification: LCC TL236.R448 2022 | DDC 629.228--dc23

Design by Richard Parsons and James Robertson

The following agencies have given permission to use their images:

Photographs supplied by the individual car manufacturers.
Additional images published with the permission of Getty.
Cover, tomas devera photo/Shutterstock.com; Cover, p. 1 Double Brain/ Shutterstock.com; pp. 3-5, 8, 9, 12, 13, 16, 17, 20, 21, 24, 25, 28-32 Carlos Caetano/Shutterstock.com.



Manufactured in the United States of America

CPSIA Compliance Information: Batch #CWPK22. For Further Information contact Rosen Publishing, New York, New York at 1-800-237-9932.

# CONTENTS

# INTRODUCTION

This book is about roadsters, and we've picked some of the most extreme ones in the world. You might wonder what made us select some but not others. Well, for a start, all the cars in this book have been, or will be, available to buy, as long as buyers have enough money and, in some cases, if they meet the conditions that the car manufacturer sets. You won't see these cars every day—and there are some that you will probably never see—but they are all out there on the world's roads or tracks somewhere!

Most of the cars are very modern and fitted with the latest technology. There are a few older cars too. However old they are, though, all the cars included have been selected because they are built to provide an incredible experience for the driver—but not necessarily for passengers. In most cases, the cars need a skilled driver to make the most of them. Some are racing cars for the road, while others are road cars that were built so that they could also be raced.

Every one of the cars included has extreme performance—either top speed or acceleration—and most are able to corner like racing cars. Of course, they all sound incredible. Some have road-car luxuries too, such as leather trim, in-car entertainment, air conditioning, and satnav.

Perhaps one day you might be lucky enough to get behind the wheel of one of the ultimate machines featured in the following pages and find out just how exciting they can be. Until then, enjoy reading and daydreaming about them!

## ABBREVIATIONS AND THEIR MEANINGS

| | |
|---|---|
| bhp | brake horsepower—available power of an engine |
| cc | cubic centimeters—volume of engine cylinders added together |
| in | inches—used for wheel sizes |
| kg | kilograms—unit of weight |
| kph | kilometers per hour—unit of speed |
| kW | kilowatts—unit of power |
| lb | pounds—unit of weight |
| lb ft | pound foot—unit of torque |
| LCD | liquid-crystal display |
| mm | millimeters—unit of length |
| mph | miles per hour—unit of speed |
| Nm | newton meter—unit of torque |
| rpm | revolutions per minute—the number of turns in one minute |
| s | seconds—unit of time |
| V6 | V-shaped engine with six cylinders (three on each side of the "V") |
| V8 | V-shaped engine with eight cylinders (four on each side of the "V") |
| V12 | V-shaped engine with 12 cylinders (six on each side of the "V") |
| W16 | W-shaped engine with 16 cylinders (four on each arm of the "W") |

## ALL ABOUT TIRES

Tires have codes that explain their sizes, and these codes are usually printed on the edge of each tire. As an example, a tire might have a code like **205/50 R15**.

| | |
|---|---|
| 205 | means that the tire is 205 mm wide. |
| 50 | means that the "profile" (thickness, or height) of the tire is 50 percent of its width. The smaller the number, the thinner the tire. |
| R | means that the tire is a "radial"-type tire—it is made from layers of material that run in layers at right angles to the direction in which the tire rolls. |
| 15 | means that the tire is designed to fit on a 15-in-diameter wheel. |

# ASTON MARTIN VALKYRIE

**A two-seater road car planned by one of the greatest F1 designers**

- Only 150 road cars and 25 track versions are planned.
- The Valkyrie AMR Pro track car is designed to lap a track as fast as an F1 car!
- The car has a special underbody design to create downforce.
- All the cars were already sold before they were built.

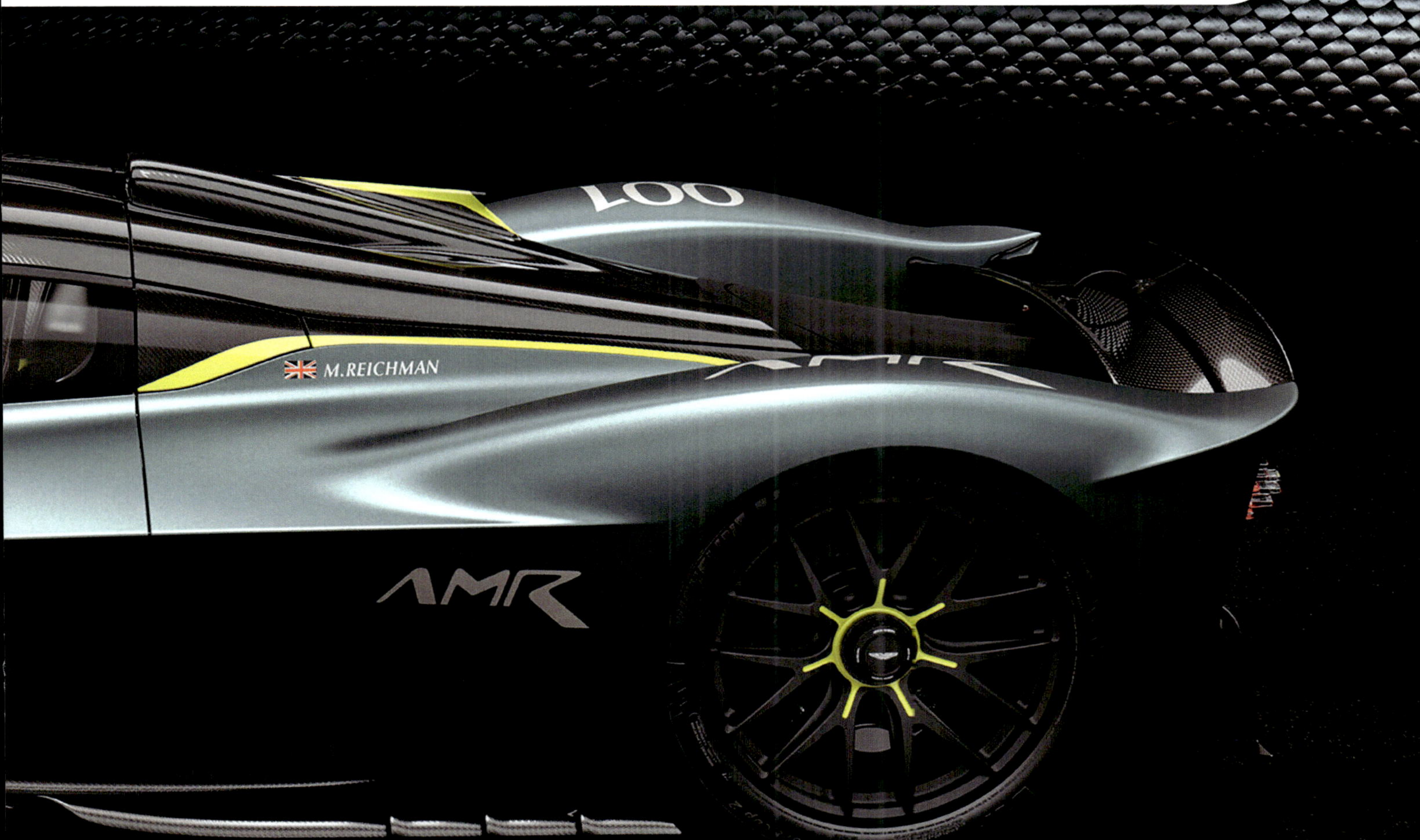

The Valkyrie is a joint project between Aston Martin and Red Bull Technology. One of the biggest selling points of the car is that Red Bull designer Adrian Newey, who has so far designed ten World Championship-winning F1 cars, has played a big part in the design. The Valkyrie is closer to a road-going F1 car than an extreme sports car.

The Valkyrie's whole structure is carbon fiber and, to save weight, not a single steel part is used in the car. Active suspension keeps the car flat to the road to improve aerodynamics. An F1-style steering wheel is supplied, with a built-in information display, and most of the car's controls are positioned on the wheel. Instead of mirrors, two rear-facing cameras are used, with displays on each side of the dashboard. The amazing V12 engine is designed to rev to 11,000 rpm and uses technology from a V8 engine that engine-building company Cosworth designed for use in F1 cars. The Valkyrie could be one of the most desirable cars ever built!

# STATISTICS ASTON MARTIN VALKYRIE

| | |
|---|---|
| Price (new) | $3 million |
| Max speed | 250 mph+ (402 kph+) |
| 0–60 mph (0–97 kph) | 2.5 s |
| Engine type | Naturally aspirated V12 developed by Cosworth |
| Engine capacity | 6.5 liters |
| Max power | 1,000 bhp (746 kW) from V12 engine, plus 160 bhp (119 kW) from KERS electric motor, giving a total of 1,160 bhp (865 kW) at 10,500 rpm |
| Max torque | 740 Nm (546 lb ft) maximum from V12, plus 280 Nm (207 lb ft) maximum from electric motor, and a combined total of 900 Nm (664 lb ft) at 6,000 rpm |
| Transmission | 7-speed paddle-shift gearbox |
| Suspension | Wishbones front and rear, with electronically controlled active ride |
| Wheels and tires | 20-in front wheels; 21-in rear wheels; 265/35 R20 front tires; 325/30 R21 rear tires |
| Curb weight | 2,425 lb (1,100 kg) |
| Length | 190 in (4,826 mm) |
| Width | 76.8 in (1,951 mm) |
| Height | 66.1 in (1,679 mm) |
| Year introduced | 2022 |

THE ASTON MARTIN BADGE ON THE NOSE IS THINNER THAN A HUMAN HAIR!

# KTM X-BOW RR

## A two-seater that looks like it belongs in a *Transformers* movie

- The X-Bow has been used in the all-star Race of Champions event since 2008.
- The quick-release steering wheel can be removed to get in and out of the car.
- Like an F1 car, it has a separate front carbon/aluminum crash structure.
- KTM recommends that a helmet is worn when driving the X-Bow.

The X-Bow (pronounced "crossbow") is built for a raw driving experience! It has a carbon-composite chassis based on a Formula 3 racing-car monocoque. There is no windscreen, or doors, but it does have two seats and a turbocharged Audi 2.0-liter 360-bhp (268 kW) engine. An optional luggage bag can be strapped to the bodywork behind the seats.

The X-Bow is the first, and so far only, car produced by Austrian motorcycle manufacturer KTM. The car has been available since 2008, and various models have been built, with the most extreme model—the RR ("Race Ready")—appearing in 2012. The RR has a more powerful engine than other models in the range, and the engine/gearbox is lowered for better weight distribution. Buyers can choose from a range of options to customize their car and its performance, including special motorsport parts. For drivers who want even more thrills, several "one-make" racing series are run especially for the X-Bow.

# STATISTICS KTM X-BOW RR

| | |
|---|---|
| Price (new) | $130,000 |
| Max speed | Approximately 145 mph (233 kph) |
| 0–62 mph (0–100 kph) | 3.3 s |
| Engine type | Audi TFSI 4-cylinder DOHC, direct injection, turbocharged with intercooler |
| Engine capacity | 1,984 cc |
| Max power | 360 bhp (268 kW) at 6,400 rpm |
| Max torque | 420 Nm (310 lb ft) at 3,200 rpm |
| Transmission | 6-speed manual gearbox, limited-slip differential |
| Suspension | Double wishbones front and rear with pushrod-operated coil spring/damper units |
| Wheels and tires | 17-in front wheels; 18-in rear wheels; 215/45 R17 front tires; 255/35 R18 rear tires |
| Curb weight | 1,786 lb (810 kg) |
| Length | 147.2 in (3,738 mm) |
| Width | 75.4 in (1,915 mm) |
| Height | 47.3 in (1,202 mm) |
| Year introduced | 2012 |

MOST OF THE CAR'S SWITCHES ARE MOUNTED ON THE STEERING WHEEL.

# LAMBORGHINI VENENO

## The most exclusive and expensive Lamborghini so far

- The Veneno is named after a famous and powerful fighting bull.
- Lamborghini kept a Veneno coupe as a birthday present to itself.
- Lamborghini developed "Rosso Veneno" paint especially for the roadster.
- At $4.5 million, the Veneno roadster costs the same as three Bugatti Veyrons!

The stunning Veneno is based on the Lamborghini Aventador but has a more powerful engine and redesigned bodywork inspired by the styling of LMP1 sports racing cars. Only three coupe and nine roadster versions have been built, taking the final number of production Venenos built to 11—pretty exclusive!

Lamborghini announced the Veneno in 2013 to celebrate the 50th anniversary of the company. The original Veneno was a coupe, and after two prototypes were built, only three production cars were made. All were sold before they were finished. The bodywork is designed to optimize the car's aerodynamics. The whole front of the car acts as a huge wing, and the flat underbody has a large downforce-producing rear diffuser, like those found on racing cars. Lamborghini announced the roadster version of the Veneno in 2014, unveiling the car spectacularly on an Italian navy aircraft carrier docked in Abu Dhabi. The Veneno roadster became the most expensive production car ever built, at $4.5 million!

# STATISTICS LAMBORGHINI VENENO

| | |
|---|---|
| Price (new) | $4.5 million [roadster] |
| Max speed | 221 mph (355 kph) |
| 0–62 mph (0–100 kph) | 2.8 s |
| Engine type | Normally aspirated V12 |
| Engine capacity | 6,498 cc |
| Max power | 750 bhp (552 kW) at 8,400 rpm |
| Max torque | 690 Nm (509 lb ft) at 5,500 rpm |
| Transmission | 7-speed semi-automatic gearbox, four-wheel-drive, mechanical limited-slip differential |
| Suspension | Double wishbones front and rear, with pushrod-operated spring/damper units |
| Wheels and tires | 20-in front wheels; 21-in rear wheels; 255/30 R20 front tires; 355/25 R21 rear tires |
| Curb weight | 3,285 lb (1,490 kg) [roadster] |
| Length | 197.6 in (5,020 mm) |
| Width | 81.7 in (2,075 mm) |
| Height | 45.9 in (1,165 mm) |
| Year introduced | 2013 |

IN 2016, A USED VENENO ROADSTER WAS AUCTIONED FOR $8.3 MILLION!

# LOTUS 3-ELEVEN 430

## A big engine in a small car for maximum excitement

- Just 20 3-Eleven 430s were built out of a total of 311 3-Eleven models.
- The 3-Eleven 430 is the fastest road-legal car ever to lap Lotus's test track.
- The car is supplied with semi-slick tires as standard.
- Built for the track, the car has just enough equipment to make it street-legal.

The Lotus 3-Eleven is the most extreme and expensive Lotus road car yet built. In early 2018, Lotus announced that the final 20 cars to be built would be upgraded "430" models. These cars are powered by a supercharged 3.5-liter, 430-bhp (321 kW) Toyota V6—a hugely powerful engine for a car as small as the 3-Eleven.

The 3-Eleven has a bonded aluminum chassis, with built-in rollover protection, and lightweight carbon-composite bodywork and interior panels. The 430 has a rear wing mounted higher up than that of the standard 3-Eleven, and a modified front splitter that increases the car's aerodynamic downforce to improve grip. Reviewers say that the 3-Eleven is one of the best-handling and most exciting sports cars ever built. The car has very basic controls—a digital display, a steering-column stalk for the signal lights and headlight main beam, a small carbon-fiber control panel that contains the starter button, fire extinguisher button, battery isolation switch, headlight, fog light, and hazard flasher switches—and that's it!

# STATISTICS LOTUS 3-ELEVEN 430

| | |
|---|---|
| Price (new) | $143,000 |
| Max speed | 180 mph (290 kph) |
| 0–62 mph (0–100 kph) | 3.2 s |
| Engine type | Toyota 24-valve V6, supercharged with intercooler |
| Engine capacity | 3,456 cc |
| Max power | 430 bhp (321 kW) at 7,000 rpm |
| Max torque | 440 Nm (325 lb ft) at 4,500 rpm |
| Transmission | 6-speed manual gearbox, limited-slip differential, variable traction control |
| Suspension | Double wishbones front and rear with adjustable dampers |
| Wheels and tires | 18-in front wheels; 19-in rear wheels; 225/40 R18 front tires; 275/30 R19 rear tires |
| Curb weight | 2,039 lb (920 kg) |
| Length | 162.2 in (4,120 mm) |
| Width | 73.2 in (1,860 mm) |
| Height | 47.2 in (1,200 mm) |
| Year introduced | 2018 |

THE "430" ADDITION TO THE NAME INDICATES 430 BHP (321 KW) POWER.

# PAGANI HUAYRA ROADSTER

The Pagani Huayra Roadster, one of the fastest roofless cars ever

- Electronic active suspension and aerodynamics keep the car stable.
- The lines visible in the carbon-fiber body panels meet in the center of the car.
- Special Pirelli P Zero Corsa tires were designed just for the Roadster.
- The car has a removable roof panel, but there is nowhere in the car to store it!

You may have heard of the Huayra BC already. The Roadster uses some of the BC's high-tech systems and materials but is a very different car. Even by hypercar standards, the lightweight parts for the Huayra Roadster are extreme, and special "Carbo-Triax" composite material is used for the bodywork. The result is a weight savings of 176 lb (80 kg) compared to the coupe!

Originally, the design of the Huayra Roadster was to be based on the coupe, with a removable roof. However, in 2013, Pagani scrapped this idea and began a completely new design for the Roadster, although the general shape is still similar to that of the coupe. The aim was to make the Roadster lighter—usually, roadster versions of a car are heavier than coupes because they need strengthening due to the lack of roof. The lightweight parts include titanium bolts used throughout the car, each with a Pagani logo and costing more than $90 a piece! The Roadster also has a more powerful engine, making it the most powerful Pagani yet built.

# STATISTICS PAGANI HUAYRA ROADSTER

| | |
|---|---|
| Price (new) | $2.6 million |
| Max speed | 238 mph (383 kph) |
| 0–60 mph (0–97 kph) | 2.8 s |
| Engine type | Mercedes-Benz AMG, twin-turbo V12 |
| Engine capacity | 5,980 cc |
| Max power | 764 bhp (562 kW) at 5,500 rpm |
| Max torque | 1,000 Nm (738 lb ft) at 2,300–4,300 rpm |
| Transmission | 7-speed automated manual transmission with electronic mechanical differential |
| Suspension | Double wishbones front and rear with front and rear anti-roll bars, coil springs, and adjustable dampers |
| Wheels and tires | 20-in front wheels; 21-in rear wheels; 255/35 ZR20 front tires; 325/30 ZR21 rear tires |
| Curb weight | 2,822 lb (1,280 kg) |
| Length | 181.3 in (4,605 mm) |
| Width | 80.2 in (2,036 mm) |
| Height | 46 in (1,169 mm) |
| Year introduced | 2017 |

JUST 100 HUAYRA ROADSTERS WERE BUILT, MADE-TO-ORDER FOR THEIR OWNERS.

# TESLA ROADSTER

**An electric roadster that could be a look into the future for extreme cars**

- Would-be owners can pre-order a car for a $50,000 deposit.
- A lightweight removable glass roof panel can be stored in the trunk.
- Tesla aims for the car to be the quickest-accelerating and fastest road car available.
- The car should have a range of 620 miles (998 km) before it needs recharging.

The original Tesla Roadster was built between 2008 and 2012, but the new Roadster that should be delivered to its first owners in 2022 is a completely new car. The Roadster is an all-electric four-seater (though the back seats are very small) and could be the fastest-accelerating road car ever!

The new Roadster had a surprise unveiling in November 2017 during the launch of a future Tesla truck (the Tesla Semi). A prototype Roadster was driven out of the back of the Semi trailer! The Roadster will be a normal production car instead of a limited-edition hypercar. The first 1,000 cars will be special "Founder's Series" cars, and anyone who wants to buy one has to pay the full price of $250,000 up front. The car has three electric motors—one at the front and two at the rear, which will give it four-wheel drive. A "SpaceX package" will include cold-air thrusters, like the SpaceX spacecraft, to improve cornering and acceleration. The Roadster could change the future for extreme cars.

## STATISTICS TESLA ROADSTER

| | |
|---|---|
| Price (new) | Base model around $200,000 |
| Max speed | Target 250 mph (402 kph) |
| 0–60 mph (0–97 kph) | Target 1.9 s |
| Engine type | Three electric motors |
| Engine capacity | Not applicable |
| Battery | 200 kilowatt hours (720 megajoules) |
| Max torque | Wheel torque—10,000 Nm (7,376 lb ft) |
| Transmission | Four-wheel drive |
| Suspension | Unknown |
| Wheels and tires | Unknown |
| Curb weight | Unknown |
| Length | 165.4 in (4,200 mm) [estimate] |
| Width | 78.7 in (2,000 mm) [estimate] |
| Height | 47.2 in (1,200 mm) [estimate] |
| Year introduced | 2022 [estimate] |

ITS "YOKE"-TYPE STEERING WHEEL IS LIKE THE CONTROL COLUMN ON A PLANE.

# GLOSSARY

**aerodynamics:** having to do with a shape that allows air to flow easily around something so it can move faster

**chassis:** steel tubes that carry the engine, seats, and other parts of a car

**dampers:** devices in a suspension system that prevent bouncing up and down

**differential:** a set of gears that transmits engine power to the wheels that allow them to turn at different speeds on turns

**hypercar:** the most superior and high-performance car available

**monocoque:** a type of vehicle structure in which the body is combined with the chassis as a single unit

**normally aspirated:** describing an internal combustion engine in which air intake depends only on atmospheric pressure

**roadster:** a car with an open body that seats two and has a folding fabric top and often a luggage compartment or rumble seat in the rear

**satnav:** a satellite-based navigation system

**suspension:** a system of springs and other devices on a car that reduces the shaking and bumping caused by uneven surfaces

**torque:** a rotating force produced by an engine's crankshaft

**transmission:** the gear that transmits power from a car or truck's engine to the wheels

# FOR MORE INFO

## BOOKS

Diaz, Julio. *Tesla Model S*. North Mankato, MN: Rourke Educational Media, 2017.

Mason, Paul. *Italian Supercars: Ferrari, Lamborghini, Maserati.* New York, NY: PowerKids Press, 2019.

Smith, Ryan. *Lamborghini*. New York, NY: AV2, 2021.

## WEBSITES

**Greatest Roadsters of All Time**
*carbuzz.com/features/greatest-roadsters-of-all-time*
Check out this list and see if you agree.

**Tesla**
*www.tesla.com/roadster*
Keep up to date on the latest news from the electric carmaker.

**What Is a Roadster?**
*www.carkeys.co.uk/guides/what-is-a-roadster*
Learn more about what makes this category of cars so special.

**Publisher's note to parents and teachers:** Our editors have reviewed the websites listed here to make sure they're suitable for students. However, websites may change frequently. Please note that students should always be supervised when they access the internet.

# INDEX